WILLIAM LAWES
The Royall Consort (old version)
edited by David Pinto

CONTENTS

INTRODUCTION		iii
CRITICAL COMMENTARY		xii

Sett no. 1

(2)	Aire [Alman]	2
(3)	Alman	4
(4)	Corant	5
(5)	Corant	7
(6)	Saraband	8

Sett no. 2

(8)	Paven	9
(9)	Aire [Alman]	12
(10)	Aire [Alman]	13
(11)	Aire [Galliard]	14
(12)	Corant	16
(13)	Saraband	17

Sett no. 3

(15)	Aire [Alman]	18
(16)	Aire [Alman]	20
(18)	Corant	21
(19)	Alman	22
(20)	Corant	23
(21)	Saraband	24

Sett no. 4

(22)	Paven	26
(23)	Aire [Alman]	28
(24)	Aire [Alman]	29
(25)	Aire [Corant]	31
(26)	Corant	32
(27)	Corant	34
(28)	Saraband	35

Sett no. 5

(29)	Aire [Paven-Alman]	36
(30)	Aire [Alman]	37
(31)	Alman	38
(32)	Corant	40
(33)	Corant	42
(34)	Aire [Morriss]	43
(35)	Saraband	44

Sett no. 6

(37)	Aire [Alman]	45
(38)	Alman	46
(39)	Corant	48
(41)	Aire [Morriss]	49

ISBN-10: 1 898131 08 2; ISBN-13: 978 1 898131 08 3. Fretwork Editions, London. General Editors: Bill Hunt & Julia Hodgson
1st edition © 1995 2nd edition © 2004, reprinted 2022

Sett no. 7

(43)	Aire [Alman]	50
(44)	Alman	52
(45)	Alman	53
(46)	Aire [Corant]	54
(47)	Corant	56
(48)	Saraband	57

Sett no. 8

(50)	Aire [Alman]	58
(51)	Alman	60
(52)	Corant	61
(53)	Corant	63
(54)	Saraband	64

Sett no. 9

(55)	Paven	65
(56)	Aire [Alman]	68
(57)	Alman	70
(58)	Corant	71
(59)	Alman	72
(60)	Corant	73
(61)	Saraband	74

Sett no. 10

(62)	Paven	75
(63)	Alman	76
(64)	Corant	78
(65)	Alman	79
(66)	Corant	81
(67)	Saraband	82

Appendix: The Miscellaneous Aires

[Sett in g]

(101)	Paven	84
(103a)	Alman	86
(103b)	Alman	87
(338)	Corant	89
(70)	Alman	90
(339a)	Corant	91
(339b)	Corant	93
(337)	Alman	95

[Sett in G]

(79)	Paven	97
(320)	Alman	100
(80)	Alman	101
(322-3)	Corant	102

[Sett in d]

(76)	Paven	104
(260)	Alman	106
(264)	Saraband	107

INTRODUCTION

The Royall Consort has a major importance for 17th-century English music, which even now is hard to appreciate as it deserves. The cause of this arose in the adverse comment of the century after its composition, and lack of availability ever since.[1] It was (or perhaps more accurately, became) a collection of unusual stamp: one of 67 dances and fantasies for strings, formed in the 1630s by William Lawes (1602–1645). It is remarkable for the outstanding quality of its music, the precedent it set for composition in suite-form, and the significant evolution it underwent during the very process of composition, which presaged similar fashionable changes in scoring in the mid-century period. Its value can be fully be assessed only by making the music itself freshly and completely available: for no portion of it was published in its own time, except in the most exiguous form in the mid-century dance-collections of John Playford, for a minimal Tr-B scoring. Its longevity in manuscript copies however, some of which preserved the full versions, was a respectable 40 years; whereafter it passed into the domain of the history books. Before going 'underground' in this way, it had been influential on the language of a whole generation of mid-century composers. Even an older man, the great John Jenkins, acknowledged the fundamental importance of Lawes' achievement by describing him after his death as 'the soule of mine and all our harmony'.[2] Without Lawes, the idiosyncratic styles of Matthew Locke, Christopher Gibbons and later writers (hence too Purcell) would have been very different. The extent to which Lawes' treatment of the scorings for the Royall Consort shaped the common coinage of theatre music from the 1650s on is yet to be decided, but it must be considerable.

The present edition aims to present the original in as full detail as practical: in its two separate main stages, which both appear to reflect the composer's intentions even as they underwent unusual modifications. The first is for 2 Trebles, Tenor and Bass with continuo (2Tr-T-B-bc; the so-called 'string-quartet' scoring); the second, which appears to have overlapped and for a time superseded it, for 2Tr-2B-bc. (This edition presents also the other extant dances for the 2Tr-T-B-bc scoring for the sake of completeness). The two are not totally comparable owing to the degree of reworking, though this does not affect on the whole the dance-forms involved. Most dance-items do preserve between the two versions a 2Tr-bc shell unchanged; some underwent slight elaboration at cadence-points. Apart though from many small and perhaps insignificant discrepancies between the two versions, quite possibly due to the fallibility of transmission through handwritten copies, there was a subtle change in emphasis. Pieces that presumably were initially intended for genuine dance-function became at least partially listeners' music. Whether this was as *tafel-musik*, or as what we would now think of as concert-repertoire proper, is impossible to tell; but it must be relevant that by the time of the work's initial formation a respectable body of Jacobean chamber music in fantasy form had accumulated, which kept its following among the amateur musicians of the educated classes, until radical shifts in taste around 1680 displaced it for good. A distinctive feature however of the reign of Charles I (1625–1649) was how little this repertoire was extended by new work: Jenkins and Lawes are the two outstanding names to be mentioned from the decade 1630–40, but few if any others come to mind. The Royall Consort, which stayed in favour for the same length of time as this previous repertoire, was in its second scoring accommodated to the pattern of the chamber's 'Grave Music' by the addition of fantasy movements, and pavans on a massy scale that, for functional purposes at least, had long since (by about 1620) well-nigh passed away. The large scale of these extra pieces was made possible by relying on the normative practice (or so it seems, from surviving partbooks) of using two theorbo lutes to supply continuo on a single basso line in unfigured stave-notation. Lawes took the opportunity that this presented in both hands; he wrote in a *freistimmig*

---

[1] Chief editions to date: No.42, Paven in *a*, in Gerald Hayes *King's Music* (1937). Nos.9–12, 19 arr. for four recorders; *William Lawes 5 Pieces from The Royal Consort* ed. Carl Dolmetsch (1958; Universal edition 12586 L). Nos.37, 39 in *Aire and Coranto* ed. Cecily Arnold (Oxford,1962; Consort Transcriptions). Appendix, aire nos.76, 260 in *Dance Suite in D minor* ed. Cecily Arnold (Oxford,n.d.). Sett no.2 entire in *William Lawes Select Consort Music* ed. Murray Lefkowitz (2/1971) = MB XXI (1963) no.18. Appendix aires nos.101, 337, 103b, in William Lawes *Pavan and Two Aires a4 in G minor* ed. Layton Ring. (1964; Universal edition 12648 L). Sett no.9 entire in facsimile, extra parts from old version ed. Gordon Dodd, Viola da Gamba Society, *Supplementary Publication* 119 (1976).

[2] Henry and William Lawes *Choice Psalmes* (1648): 'An Elegiack Dialogue on the sad loſse of his much esteemed Friend, Mr. William Lawes, servant to his Majesty'. The words are put in the mouth of an interlocutor who may be Henry Lawes; but Jenkins was the setter of the sentiment.

contrapuntal style that took full advantage of the potential six-part scoring (not to mention his reliance on the virtuoso performers who comprised his fellow-servants) in two ways: either to deliver 6-part counterpoint or to coalesce into as few as three real parts and emphasise basic elements in the texture. For its times, this riposte to the demands (or the constraints) of scoring seems to be more or less unique.[3] The fantasies and pavans are comparable in terms of procedures to those he was writing more or less contemporaneously for six viols and organ, and deserve to be viewed in a similar way, as embodiments of all that the self-regard of court culture by the end of the 1630s found as most noble and permanent in itself.

The modern study of the Royall Consort, and of the works of William Lawes in general, owes most to the research of Murray Lefkowitz as contained in his academic studies, subsequently published (principally as a monograph covering the composer's life and works), and his editions of this composer's music, which include the second sett entire as a taste of the whole. The valuable assessments by predecessors, in particular Rupert Erlebach and Ernst Hermann Meyer should not be forgotten; but Professor Lefkowitz comprehensively listed the then-known sources and mapped out the *genres* that Lawes employed. He established the existence of two chief forms for the Royall Consort, and identified their presence in the composer's holograph scorebook, one of a pair that have reposed in the collection of Oxford's Music School since the later 17th century. His division of the sources into 'old' and 'new' was amplified and—bating further discoveries—completed in the *Thematic Index of Music for Viols,* compiled by Gordon Dodd for the Viola da Gamba Society of Great Britain. (Designations 'old' and 'new' are by the way modern, since no contemporary source apart from one important one, now fragmentary, seems to have copied both versions side by side). Together with Cdr Dodd's own comparative assessment of the sources, these studies and the contents of the sources themselves are the basis for any following edition; building on these findings, a few conclusions can it is hoped be sketched here, aided by summary reference to associated remarks published elsewhere.

Each item of the opus, as it has become recognised in modern times, has received a through-numbering in a series 1–67 as a result of the assessment of the sources referred to previously, starting from the sequence found in the composer's scorebook. Collectively they divide fairly naturally into 10 setts, each of 6–7 pieces. The *genres* included are Paven (including Paven-Alman), Galliard, Alman, Corant, Saraband, Morriss, Ecco, Fantazy, to use a consistent spelling based on the composer's own (the pieces are referred to here also by initial). Both the composer and the many copyists use the general term 'aire' for pieces of A, C, G and M form indiscriminately; the exact dance-type is rarely unclear. The term aire is found also in other contexts (where it is used by Lawes among others) to mean a light contrapuntal piece of fantasy type, but none occurs in this. The old version lacks piece nos.1, 36 (F), 7, 40 (E), 42, 49 (P), for reasons connected with the rescoring process. It also omits no.14 (S) and 17 (C) for no obvious reason, but perhaps fortuitously, since these are not items that exploit the paired scoring. Eleven more of the old version's pieces survive in a fragmentary state, which can be patched by reference to the new version. The new version lacks only one piece found in the old, no.27 (C), again for unknown reasons.[4]

The setts of dances found in the Royall Consort mark the beginning of suite-form in England for any scoring: by suite is meant the aggregated chain of Alman-Corant-Saraband, to which the Jig was shortly added. In this form it persisted into the high baroque as part of a living tradition, however attenuated eventually became its contact with performed dance. It seems that Paris, and the publications of lutenists, mark the first coalescence of the suite by the year 1629; but Lawes and his colleagues in the service of English royalty were not far behind.[5] Their A-C-S sequences, for some instrumentation or other, could be as early as 1630; and it would be unlikely on evidence available from the musical sources to put them even as much as 5 years later. The Royall Consort itself is the chief evidence for the moment when such sequences formed in England, apart from contemporary work by colleagues of Lawes like Charles Coleman and William Drew; but at first

---

[3] One minor exception is in a set of paperbound partbooks, now Lcm 1146: 'Consort./ For 2 Treble Viollins / 2 Bases and 2 Theorboes', a multi-sectional and rather puzzling piece of no appreciable merit. Works, of comparable stature to those of Lawes, by Jenkins for 2Tr-2B rely on organ continuo—score in *Musica Britannica* (= *MB*) XXVI, *John Jenkins Consort Music of Four Parts* ed. Andrew Ashbee (1969 2/1975) nos.1–32.

[4] The present edition reverses numeration for nos.27–8 as found in the *Thematic Index of Music for Viols* i–vi ed. Gordon Dodd (1980–1992), in order to give a more usual position for the (final) saraband in sett no.4.

[5] David Fuller 'Suite', in *The New Grove* (1980) = *Grove's Dictionary of Music and Musicians* (6th edn), contains a succinct and comprehensive study of the suite's formative period.

there may well have been nothing codified to insist on definite suites within the 'orders', other than the call from the dance-floor by the master of ceremonies. Orders did shortly begin to form, and were standard within twenty years. Some early evidence for a preferential order is found in the composer's score; as it happens the clearest and most logical source in setting out an order for the pieces that he wrote in it (only three-fifths of the whole, as it chances). It shows that Lawes had already inserted the occasional jig into the sequence, if the synonymity of the terms jig, morris and country dance can be accepted (for there seem to be no fast distinctions to be made between them on grounds of metre, or form). The catalyst in establishing the suite was apparently the saraband, which had been known in England (by its first literary reference) in 1617, but was probably for a decade longer usually played on single (principally plucked) instruments, or extemporised by small groups of added melody instruments, in keeping with its popular origin.[6] Sources for lute and keyboard which might throw further light on this development are unfortunately absent over the relevant period 1620–1630. While the saraband was being incorporated, the pavan may, not entirely coincidentally, have dropped out of the danced repertoire completely. The pavans of the Royall Consort belong on the whole to its later manifestation, and can therefore be considered as primarily audience-music. Exceptions which are present in the old version and seem to show its continued use may all fall into a slightly different category, that of 'pavan-alman'. The term is used by Playford in his popular dance-publications; it also occurs in manuscript collections. Pavan-almans combine the harmonic pace of a pavan with melodic detail more typical of the alman, and are mostly (but not all) in binary form—in two strains. This cross-form may derive from tendencies in the Jacobean dance, though the practice probably preceded the name for it. The remaining common dance-forms of the Royall Consort, alman and corant, are not in themselves problematic, and show a continuity with past and future examples. The editor however is of the opinion that the musical boundary between corant and saraband is not so great as to disallow occasional practical use of one as the other; at least contemporary MSS occasionally exhibit confusion over nomenclature, which is best accounted for by variation in dance-practice. (It follows that no standard speeds can be set for dances, most of which seem to evolve divergent *tempi* early in their history). The 'eccos' are character corants, devised to show off the dualism of the new scoring (two Tr-B pairs); they are the less likely to have been intended for dance. The fantasies also have no dance-function as such unless they just possibly were preludial summons to dancers; into a like category could fall the elaborate real pavans of the new version. It is clear however from contemporary usage, maintained into the Commonwealth period in new work by Matthew Locke among others, that the pavan was regarded as natural head of a formal sequence, P-A-C-S, which can hardly be considered complete without it.[7] The galliard also was not forgotten entirely and held an honorific place following the pavan on occasion.[8] No dances exhibit the change in metre that was a characteristic of choreographed masque dances, apart from one in the appendix of miscellaneous aires (no.260); all others are apparently intended for regular, 'social', dancing, possibly in the revels of the court.

The main partbook copies of the old version contain two other preceding setts in the same scoring, which circumstances somehow conspired to render ineligible for recasting in a new form for 2Tr-2B. This series of P-A-C aires in keys g-G overlaps with other less well-considered groupings elsewhere; such as those found in the miscellaneous sets of dances transcribed into manuscript (Och 367–370) by the collector John Browne in the mid-1630s, and in sequences of aires from time to time added to a collection from the possession of the Shirley family, later Earls Ferrers, of Staunton Harrold, Leicestershire, in the composer's own hand (now Lbl Add. MSS 40657–40661). The g-G series was quarried by the composer for other purposes: items were rearranged for 5 viols and organ, or for 2 division bass viols and organ, which are all found in his holograph scores (lacking just the organ parts to the viol consorts). The series has limited connection to the Royall Consort proper (for a start, it contains no sarabands), but must be included with it as a record of the

---

[6] Ben Jonson *The Divell is an Asse,* IV *iv* 164, acted 1617, is the first reference to the dance; but it was not published until the collected edition of 1631, giving rise to probably unjustified suspicion that mention was added on revision. See also *The Staple of Newes* IV *ii* 133 'the bawdy Saraband' (also published 1631).

[7] Matthew Locke *Chamber Music I–II* ed. Michael Tilmouth (1971–2) = *MB* XXXI–XXXII, *passim*.

[8] Ob MS Mus Sch.D.220 is a prime example of a large and comprehensive MS collection from the same (Commonwealth) period, listing in its title 'Pavanes Galliardes Ayres Almains Coranto's Sarabands Moriscas Maskes & Contry-Dances'. Similar hierarchies are expressed by printed order and titles of John Playford's contemporary publications: see Robert Thompson *English Music Manuscripts and the Fine Paper Trade* (Ph.D dissertation, University of London,1988).

composer's development in the 'old' scoring. To this annexe are appended three remaining dances in key d, for the sake of completing the extant output of William Lawes in the one scoring. Of these, the second is the only dance here included to exhibit change of metre (from duple to triple), the alman-corant no.260 mentioned above. The last of them is a widely-copied saraband that has only a tenuous claim to be by Lawes: it is not especially characteristic of his writing, and is attributed in only one peripheral source out of the known six. One of the main sources for the old version contains further unattributed aires thought in modern times to be possibly also by Lawes. They are however so untypical that the ascription to Thomas Brewer, actually found in the other main source for the old version, should be accepted; no further comment is made on them here.[9] The Shirley books contain other fantasy-aires for 2Tr-T-B, and dances for 2Tr-2B in the composer's hand. Two of these fantasy-aires were included by the composer in a group of pieces divisible into two consort setts in c-C in his autograph score; but these are outside the scope of a genuine dance-collection, and not included herein.[10]

A reason for the decision to rescore the old version entire was given in a prefatory note to his copies by Edward Lowe, Heather Professor of Music at Oxford (in succession to Lawes' colleague, the lutenist John Wilson) from 1661 until his death in 1682:

> The followinge Royall Consort was first composd for
> 2 Trebles a Meane & a Base. but because the Middle
> part could not bee performd with equall advantage to bee
> heard as the trebles were. Therfore the Author involved
> the Inner part in two breakinge Bases: which I
> causd to bee transcribd for mee in the Tenor & Counter
> -tenor Bookes belonginge to thes. & soe bound. Wher the
> two breakinge Bases are to be found. & soe many
> figured as agree with thes in Order/.   (Mus.Sch.MS D.236)

Problems arise when the implications of this apparently straightforward explanation are pursued. Why, as Gordon Dodd remarked, should it matter if the inner voice in dance-music is not heard distinctly? It is strange too that Lowe's remarks precede a selection of the dances from the old version—for though his partbooks for lines III–IV are now lost, this much is clear from the unrevised state of the remaining lines, even if Lowe did later make them more comprehensive by adding the revised parts. His words are not a simple endorsement of the new version's superiority; they could even imply a preference for the old, in accordance with his known antipathy to common musicians such as violinists, a foible not vanquished until the later commonwealth period.[11] When the musical texture of the old version is scrutinised, a further oddity is plain: the tenor line for an appreciable part of its time makes very little attempt at independence, and indulges in much parallel movement at the octave or even unison with the outer lines. It is inconceivable that this extreme practice was not deliberate, in a collection of this scale, even if the composer later decided to cultivate a more orthodox polyphony that he had earlier flouted. A change in function, character, or style of performance (such as an altered place of performance), or all of these must be behind the rescoring process; alternatively, the change could have been demanded of a royal servant, in a manner that he was unable to refuse. However, it does appear (from the musical text once more) that a shift in style occurs between setts nos. 1–6 in d-D, as found revised in the composer's scorebook, and the remainder, which follows a more varied key-sequence, and also conforms internally to a more orderly pattern in exclusion of the more unusual movements (E, F, G, M) and inclusion of introductory P (or possibly P-A). There is in this remainder a fuller

---

[9] Murray Lefkowitz *William Lawes* (1960) 75–6; *MB* XXI p.xix. The claim has been accepted and the pieces have been accordingly listed in *Thematic Index*, Lawes nos.215–218, 239–242, 308–310, 329–333, 371–377, from Ob MSS Mus.Sch.F.568–9; from where they should be removed and reassigned to Brewer on the strength of the ascribed complete versions in Mus.Sch. E.431–6.

[10] See Lawes, *Suite no.1 in C Minor and Suite no.2 in C major* ed. Richard Taruskin (Ottowa,1983); the same setts ed. Richard Nicholson with an editorial organ part supplied, *English Consort Series* xiv (1985). Most of the other aires in four parts have been published in the *Supplementary Publications* Series of the Viola da Gamba Society, nos.5, 8, 20, 34, 75. Aire no.319 lacks a treble part in the unique source, the Shirley Partbooks; a restored version with editorial cantus part (line I) was included in *SP* 20.

[11] See Pinto 'Debatable territory in the Royall Consort' (in preparation); Ian Woodfield 'The First Earl of Sandwich, a Performance of William Lawes in Spain and the Origins of the Pardessus de Viole' *Chelys* xiv (1985) 40–2.

use made of independent lines in the 4-part texture; which is apparent in both old and new forms. For these and other reasons internal to the sources, such as more variegated order between copies of the *d-D* setts, and a greater regularity in the transmission of the remainder, it becomes clear that Lowe's evidence cannot strictly be taken to apply to the Royall Consort as a whole.[12] (He copied only *d-D* aires). It is also clear that the transition to a new scoring began after the completion (or near-completion) of the *d-D* 'ordres', but before composition of the remainder. The old and new versions for the later setts, that is, were written in parallel and not consecutively. After these had been worked out together, the very latest of the pieces added probably were those devised for the new version only, the Fantazy and Ecco pieces in the *d-D* setts nos.1 and 6.

TEXT

In establishing a sound text of the Royall Consort as a whole, it follows that there is no guaranteeable *stemma* along a standard path of linear descent (old-autograph-new, that is, with primacy given to the autograph where available); instead a triangular relationship subsists, without an inferrable clear temporal direction. The old and new can at times concur against the autograph score; mainly in 'accidental' rather than 'substantive' features. For most purposes this is of little significance, given the authority inherent in a composer's score; exceptions are noted below. The Royall Consort was obviously popular in its day; in varying degrees of completeness there survive two sources for the old version, six chief sources for the new (excluding from the count the autograph score, and partial selections like Lowe's). No one source is directly dependent for its text on another, though some are fairly closely related; which implies a substantial background of copies now lost. There is therefore a strong possibility that newly rediscovered sources will yet emerge from time to time[13]. For the old version this edition is based on a comparison of all sources, which are of similar value and can provide mutual corrections. 'Old' pieces now lacking parts are completed editorially, by comparison with the new version. For the new version, priority is given to the composer's score for setts nos.1–6 (source D) and for the rest the well-connected set of partbooks Och 754–759 (source G), which is the most generally accurate and complete of the copies. Even these two sources, as copytexts, require the occasional minor correction. The musical texts as printed are therefore strictly speaking conflates. They may however be taken generally to represent the copytexts, since all additions to and divergences from them are noted in the accompanying critical commentary, apart from diacritical signs like added ties and slurs and editorial accidentals, which are indicated on the page.

SOURCES

The sources of mid-17th-century dance-collections are to date not studied with that exhaustive treatment afforded to the fantasy literature; and there is correspondingly less that can be said with assurance. Cataloguing is at present under way of the two main libraries for MS copies of the Royall Consort, the Bodleian Library and Christ Church, both in Oxford. The main sources have a clear pedigree. For the new version, source D, the composer's autograph score, has been housed in the Music School collection at Oxford University since the later 17th century. Source G has been at Christ Church Oxford for a comparable length of time; it was given by bequest from the collection of the college's dean, Henry Aldrich, in 1710, and may have been in his possession since 1670, a likely date for its acquisition along with other music from the same source. Since that source was the family collection of Baron Hatton, a veteran of the king's Oxford court, there is a fighting chance that the text represents wartime usage *c*.1642–6; but this is speculation in the absence of collateral records. On internal grounds alone it seems trustworthy, and gives the text with what appear to be

---

[12] There is a larger number of pieces making up the 2 *d-D* orders than the 4 other setts (41, against 26). They are also more widely broadcast in the miscellaneous and later sources than setts nos.7–10, which suggests that these last never circulated independently as single dances.

[13] See Richard Charteris, 'A rediscovered manuscript source...' *Chelys* xxii (1993) 3–29, for aires nos. 79 and 320, as found in the annexe to the old version, apparently rescored for the 2Tr-2B combination, alongside an alman from the violin setts, aire no 118 (the source is incomplete, and scoring is not certain).

its latest additions.[14] Principal sources for the old version are three in number: two (sources A, B) made for use in the Oxford Music School at about the time that tuition resumed there in 1657; a third (source F) being a partial selection housed in the same collection, which was copied in the hand of the Professor of Music there at some time post-Restoration, luckily from an independent source.[15] None of the other sources for old or new version has the same intrinsic worth as these, but collectively they serve to validate or refute the evidence of the main manuscripts.

TITLING

The general designation of 'The Royall Consort' is widespread in partbook copies: found in sources C, F, G (in a later hand), J and K. 'Old' version sources (principally A, B) do not carry a title—nor for that matter do the autograph scores (D, E). Other non-extant sources are known to have used the title: one belonging in 1667 to Sir Peter Leycester was catalogued as 'The Royall Consort by Will:Lawes, for 4 violes, with a Continued Basse ...'.[16] Other divergent titles of note are 'Flat Ayres' and 'Sharp Ayres' in source F, which hints at an early origin in two undifferentiated orders for the majority groups in d-D; the earlier if subsidiary title in G, 'm^r william lawes his Consort', and H, 'Mr Lawes his Great Consort'. It is hard to credit that the main title would have been so egregiously chosen by the composer, or any of his associates, since it smacks of an ostentation foreign to the native way of indicating superior status. Equally, it is unlikely to be a term applied exclusively to the scoring as such, either in its earlier or in its later 2Tr-2B shape, since neither can have been thought of as a specific prerogative of royal musicians. The 'old version' as represented in source F carries the designation too, though possibly out of hind-knowledge of the new. The usage of 'consort' to mean a written collection of music is not one known to the *Oxford English Dictionary*, though there is no proof that this particular collection was the first to bear it; and it was used extensively by Matthew Locke in his mid-century setts such as 'The Little Consort', whereby a reference to the *scale* of a work, as well as some other feature of scoring, is confirmed. The title does though appear to belong to a primary level of dispersal of the music, and must refer to usage within the royal court as seen from without; but whether this occurred in wartime conditions or in the period immediately preceding war cannot be told. Separate titling for setts does not occur in the sources, and they are a modern convenience which can if thought fit be ignored in selecting items for combination. Similarly with the three setts of aires in the appendix: the first two have a corporate identity through grouping in the sources, but the third is a totally chance collocation of a connected P-A group with a single S of less certain authorship.

Titling of single movements follows the composer's preferred spellings as found in setts 1–6 (excepting only 'Saraband', expanded from the contracted 'Sarab~d'). Setts 7–10, which do not occur in the composer's autograph (source D), have a musical text based on source G, but spelling of the titlings it gives has been altered to concur with the composer's. Many aires were given the unspecific label of 'aire', whether in duple or triple metre; one source for example (source I) gives no other titling to almans. Added titles (from whatever source) are distinguished from those of the copytexts by enclosure in square brackets. The partbook copies do not always agree on titling for the more unusual pieces. As with the unspecified 'aires', the forms are usually self-evident; dissension between sources is noted in the accompanying critical commentary. The more methodical sources do contain their own through-numbering system for pieces, but these all differ to some degree. The standard modern numeration is followed here, except for a re-ordering with piece nos.27–28 (see above, footnote 4).

---

[14] Apart from the Bodleian Library's *Catalogue of Music* ed. M. Crum and others (in progress), the chief sources for information about source D are in Murray Lefkowitz *William Lawes* (1960); William Lawes *Consort Sets* ed. Pinto (1979) and *id. Fantasia-Suites* ed. Pinto (1991)=*Musica Britannica* LX. For source G see Pinto 'The music of the Hattons' *Royal Musical Association Research Chronicle* xxiii (1990) 79–108.

[15] Bodleian Library *Catalogue of Music*. A date in mid-Commonwealth period is most probable for sources A, B judging by the use in ascribing music to Charles Coleman of the title of doctor, the degree he took on 2nd July 1651.

[16] Reference to another lost source was unearthed by Richard Andrewes from a 17th-century catalogue of the Chapter House Library, Gloucester Cathedral: see Frank Traficante 'Music for the Lyra Viol ...' *Chelys* viii (1978–9) 4–22. This last also contains details of the Leycester MS, for which see also Sir Peter Leicester *Charges to the Grand Jury at Quarter Sessions 1660–1677* ed. Elizabeth M. Halcrow (Manchester,1953) and John M. Ward *Sprightly and Cheerful Musick = Lute Society Journal* xxi (1979–81).

INSTRUMENTATION

The scoring of the new version is specified by the composer in MS Mus.Sch. B.3: 2 violins, 2 bass viols and 2 theorbos. The bowed strings have standard tunings for bass viol and violin. Occasionally bass viols touch on low C, but this was probably effected by retuning the 6th string (D) down a tone. (See piece no.1 bar 22, no.49 bars 26, 35, 76, no.56 bar 26, no.57 bars 2, 7, 27). It is not yet clear what type of 'theorbo' lute was fashionable at the time, in the absence of surviving instruments. At least 11 courses are required to realise fully any single sett out of the whole, allowing for retuning between setts. Never less than three, never more than five diapason strings are required in any one sett: giving in combination a total of eight different pitches (see table). For the range of types of theorbo available, see Linda Sayce's note on the topic.[17] The theorbos

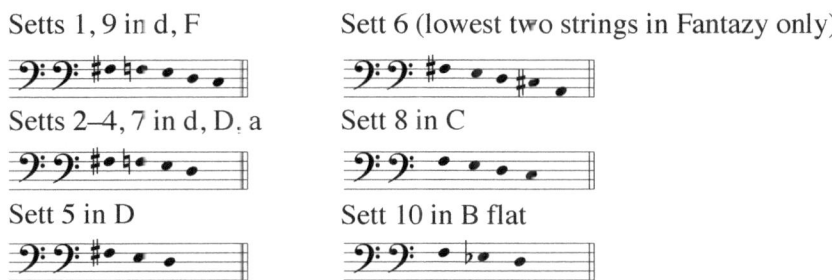

read from ordinary stave-notation, which could imply that contrapuntal lines rising to written a' (no.1 bar 11) involved strings capable of achieving written pitch, and therefore containing at least one member of the pair in the first two courses (nominal d' and a) tuned so rather than an octave lower. Two theorbos appear to be a standard continuo grouping in both the old and new versions, though only the new makes separate use of them. It is also allowably authentic to omit this hand-plucked continuo and substitute harpsichord. The practice may postdate Lawes by a decade, but is attested in copies (of what may have been the 'old version') belonging to Sir Peter Leycester; it also is confirmed by Thomas Mace as general practice in the performance of the 'jocond' side of the chamber repertoire.[18] For the interchangeability of continuo instruments, one can view the prescriptions of respected composers in their holograph parts and scores who regarded organ and harpsichord to some extent as acceptable alternatives. George Jeffreys wrote his 3-part fantasies 'for ye Violls and the Virginall', but then described extra continuo notes, placed in the stave given to line III, as for organ (Lbl Add.MS 10338 f.4, and following musical text). John Hingeston wrote a lone 'Fantazia for one Violin, Baſe Viol, a Pedall Harpsichord, or Organ' (Ob Mus.Sch.MS E.382 p.74). However continuo is realised, it should be noted that in the 'old version' and in dances of its appendix, the tenor part (line III) often dips below the notated level of continuo. From this alone it appears that constant doubling on the diapason strings at the lower octave must have been the duty of at least one theorbo out of the pair, at any one time. The practice can be seen at work in the observations on playing a theorbo part, and the examples given, in Thomas Mace's treatise of 1676.[19] No source contains figuring apart from a single occurrence in the composer's score (to piece no.36). The extra role demanded of the theorbos in the 'new' fantasy movements, of adding to the polyphonic texture, does not exempt them from constantly being on the *qui vive* for opportunities to embellish, and add harmonies *ad libitum*. In the old version, any separate continuo part that may once have existed had disappeared, except in a few small details, before extant copies were made. In a few essential places editorial passages have been suggested for continuo use alone, which are distinguished from original divergent lines by enclosure within brackets; they may of course be ignored.

---

[17] Linda Sayce 'Performing Purcell: A Question Answered' *EMR* viii (March,1995) 4–15.
[18] See Traficante 'Music for the Lyra Viol...', and Ward *Sprightly and Cheerful Muſick* for Leycester; Thomas Mace *Musick's Monument* (Cambridge and London,1676) 235.
[19] Mace (1676) part 2 chapter xliii, especially pp.221–230.

The type of treble instrument used in the old version is never specified by sources. Players can feel free to use treble viols as an alternative to violins for four reasons:

(1) In the context of the chamber music to which the pieces by origin belong, there is no reason to think that violins would have been granted a prerogative right to play even dance music.

(2) One can assume that professional players were competent on both families of instrument, where even amateur players seemingly could deal with technically demanding repertoire on the treble viol.[20]

(3) Viols would almost certainly have been preferred by the Oxford circles that preserved the 'old version' in the mid-1650s.

(4) Treble viol as an equivalent for violin is mentioned as late as 1651 in an advertisement placed for a practical new dance-collection, Playford's *The English Dancing Master*.[21]

The treble viol may have been superseded shortly after 1660, but before that date there is no good reason to deny it its fair share of glory in realising this repertoire. The family of the tenor instrument used in the old version is never specified. The total range is large, from A (lowest space of the bass clef) in piece no.26, up to d" in piece no.60. Assuming that one type of instrument is employed, then ordinary viola seems to be out of the running; and the problems in assigning this type of line to the so-called 'tenor violin' are unresolved.[22] It seems best to suggest that tenor viol was employed in normal conditions.

EDITORIAL PROCEDURE

Original note-values, clefs and time-signatures are retained; excepting only that clef-changes between F4 and C3 in basses and theorbos have been systematised in hopes of clarifying phrasing and avoiding excessive clef-change. Occasional notes supplied editorially, including extra continuo notes in the old version where there is a possibility that some may have been lost, are enclosed in square brackets, but when whole parts are supplied for non-extant lines, notice of the completion is kept to the commentary. Where the two parts occur together on the stave, the theorbo is the lower, with descending stems. Original sharp and flat are replaced by modern natural where appropriate, and modern enharmonic equivalents replace unsystematic accidentals. Other editorial accidentals, when either supplementary or corrective in effect, are placed above the stave and the note concerned; they apply to one note only, except that they continue to have force within a single beamed group of notes.

One editorial change of metre from quadruple to duple, ¢ (= 4/2) to 4/4, and back again, occurs in no.36 (F in *D*). Regular barring is introduced throughout. The composer's scorebook was pre-ruled and does not conform to a methodical system of barring. No sets of parts originally were barred, although barring was sometimes added later, as in source I. Some irregular (*i.e.* short) bars will be found without admonitory change of time-signature, in P, C, S, E forms. Apart from this, lengths of final notes are regularised without other notification; final pause-marks have been excluded. Double bars to indicate customary repeats are introduced. The method of transition to repeated or following sections follows that of the composer, which conforms to contemporary standard practice where 'second-time' alternative bars at section-ends, to systematise durations, are rarely found. As a result, those dances with an anacrusis at section-beginnings will sometimes be found to be short or long by a fraction of a note-beat. Since the intent is always clear, the simplest way of showing it is by refraining from unnecessary insertions; the general editors concur in finding this a practical method, easily comprehended by players. Bars are through-numbered, but anacruses are taken to belong to the preceding whole bar: thus for purposes of numbering the initial upbeat is bar 0, and the upbeat following a double-bar does not form a new bar in itself. Abbreviations used in the critical commentary are as follows: Lines of the score are numbered from I–VI, uppermost down; bc = basso continuo. Pitches are

---

[20] See the demanding variations 'A Devision for a trible violl to play wth a virginall', = Barafostus' Dreame: Lbl Add.MS 36661 f.57r-v, printed as *MB* IX no.95; also the fingerings for treble viol in parts belonging to the North family for Jenkins' 2Tr-B-organ setts as preserved in Ob MS Mus.Sch. C.86: *Seven Fancy-Ayre Division Suites* ed.Robert A. Warner rev. Andrew Ashbee (2/1993).
[21] In *A Musicall Banquet* (1651), *The English Dancing Master* is advertised as 'to be played on the Treble Violl or Violin'. All editions after the first however specify violin. See *Playford's English Dancing Master 1651* ed. Margaret Dean-Smith (F/1957); *The Complete Country Dance Tunes from Playford's Dancing Master (1651–ca.1728)* ed. Jeremy Barlow (1985).
[22] Most recently see Ephraim Segerman 'The Name "Tenor Violin"' *Galpin Society Journal* xlviii (1995) 181–7, answering Agnes Kory 'A Wider Role for the Tenor Violin?' *ibid*. xlvii (1994) 123–153.

recorded in octave C–B, then c–b c'–b' c"–b" c'", where c' is middle c Durations are written as: br = breve, sbr = semibreve, m = minim, cr = crotchet, qu = quaver, squ = semiquaver; d- = dotted; and miscellaneous: extra = simultaneously present, k-s = key-signature, o = no accidental, om = omitted, transf = transferred, t-s = time-signature. Each comment is printed as Line [roman numeral] Bar(s) Mensural symbol(s) within bar, including rests Reading of variant source (Source, by alphabetical sign) /. Many less significant variants and errors are not listed; in particular, supplementary sources for dances of the appendix are lightly covered, since they offer so little of authority in establishing the original form of the pieces concerned.

Abbreviations used for holding libraries and institutions, in the notes above and the commentary below, are those of *RISM*, as follows: Ctc for Cambridge, Trinity College, and Cul University Library; Lbl for London British Library, and Lcm Royal College of Music; Nyp for New York Public Library; Ob for Oxford Bodleian Library, and Och Christ Church; T for Tenbury (now housed at Ob).

ACKNOWLEDGEMENTS

The editor is indebted to the governing bodies of the libraries mentioned below in the table of sources for access to and freedom to copy and collate the sources contributing to a complete edition. Effecting a full transcription has owed most to the ready help of Layton Ring, in offering loan of his own transcriptions and facsimile material, and the benefit of his life-long experience in bringing this music—as both played and danced—to a new life. A complete transcription of the 'new version' into publishable form was made early on by Richard Boothby from a variety of transcriptions, in association with the general editors, which group-effort lightened what otherwise would have been an insupportable chore. Julia Hodgson and Bill Hunt have in addition offered constant advice about contestable issues, from their own involvement with the music as performers. Their opinions have been often sought, and gladly deferred to, on many questions of style as well as presentation.

THE ROYALL CONSORT Old Version: Critical Commentary
(2Tr-T-B-bc)

SOURCES

A) Ob 431-6; B) Ob 568-9; D) Ob B.3; E) Ob B.2; F) Ob D.233-4,236, E.451; M) Lbl Add.31429. Additional miscellaneous aires only, in P) Wells 5-6; T) Och 367-70; U) Lbl Add.18940-4; W) Lbl Add.40657-61

Differences between continuo partbooks in the same set (in Source A, 435-6; in Source F, D.236, E.451) are notated by siglum for source followed by partbook number: e.g., (F236), (F451)

Sett no.1 in d (lacks nos.1,7)

Source B (I,III only; II,IV-V editorial)

3. I 11.1-4 om/ I 12.4-5 extra 4qu e"a'd"e"/ I 13 corona / I 17.4 c'" - see New Version/ I 18-19 differs from New

4. III 5 7th higher; misreading from original clef (C3 for F4)?

5. I 12.1 m cr f"d"/ I 13.5-8 cr d-cr qu f'e'd'/ I 14 d'

6. I 4.3-4 2qu

Sett no.2 in d (lacks no.14)

8. Sources A,B,F
B) has I,III only/ V 3.1-2 tie (F236)/ V 3.2-3 tie (F451)/ III 5.6,8.4,12.5,14.6 o (A)/ V 5.2-3 sharp natural (F451)/ V 10.7,11.1 o (F)/ V 11.1 o (F451)/ I 14.4-5 2qu (F)/ III 15.4 o (B)/ V 18.1 o (F236)/ III 19.1-2 a'g' (A) g'f' (B)/ I 20.15-16 2qu (A,B,F)/ II 21.9,22.1 o (F)/ III 23.2-3 2cr (F)/ III 28.4 flat, perhaps added later (F)/ III 29.5 o (F)/ I 32 om slurs (B,F)/ all 34 sbr (A,B)

9. Sources B,F
B) has II-III only, F has I-II,IV/ V 1-2 (lower notes) editorial/ III 8.2 e' (F)/ V 15.2 o (F)/ I 17.4 e' (F)/ V 20.3 o (F)

10. Sources A,B,F,M
B) has I,III only/ II 4.2 a' (M)/ V 4 sbr (A435-6) d-m 2qu (M)/ V 5 m-rest cr-rest 2qu (A435-6,F) cr 2qu cr 2qu (M)/ II 11 o (M)/ I 12.3,5 sharp (M)/ II 12.4 sharp (M)/ I 18.1 'drag' (B)/ I 20.1 natural (M)

11. Sources B,F,M
B) has II-III only/ note-values halved (F,M)/ III 2,4,6, 12,16 om coronae (B)/ II 5.1 m-rest m (M)/ II 5.3-4 m sbr (M)/ I 6.2-3 2m (M)/ I,II,V 8.1-3 om (F,M)/ I 8.5-6 sbr c" (M)/ all 9-10 F,M), which seem to have discarded line III, therefore excise unneeded rests/ I 9.3-10.1 om rests (F,M)/ II 9.3-10.2 om rests (F,M)/ V 9.3-10.1 om (M)/ V 10.1 m f (F,M)/ II 10.4-5 d-cr qu (F)/ I 12.4 e" (F,M)/ II 14.3 o (F)/ V 17.4 A (F) a (M)

12. Sources A,B,F,M
B) has I,III only/ I 1.7 o (A,B,M)/ II 2.1 sharp (M)/ II 2.7 o (A,M)/ all 3 d-m only (A,B,F,M)/ III 6.1 c' sharp (A,B)/ II 7.3 o (A,M)/ II 8.4 o (A,F)/ II 9.3-4 om slur (A,M)/ V 9.2 sharp, transferred from .4? (M)/ IV-V 9.4 om natural (A,M)/ II 15 om slur (A,M)/ II 17.2,18.2 sharp (M)

13. Sources A,B,F,M
B) has I,III only/ II 5.2 2cr g"a" (F)

Sett no.3 in d (lacks no.17)

Sources A,B (I,III only),F

15. I 4.4 o (F)/ II 7.1 o (A)/ II 8.1-2 2qu (A) d-qu squ (F)/ II 8.1-4 2dqu-squ (A)/ II 11.4-5 2cr (A)/ IV-V 15-16 om tie (A)/ II 25 sbr-rest (A,F) sbr a" (B)/ IV 31.2 fo (A434)/ I 32.2-3 2qu (A,F) d-qu squ (B)

16. I 10.2 o (F)/ II 12.6-7 b' flat c" (A)/ III 12.2-3 m a' (A) 2cr a' a (B)/ V 15.2-16.2 m d-m (F451)/ I 19.3-4 2qu (B)/ II 19.1-2,5-6 om slur (A)/ II 19.8 o (F)

17. M) carries a version of this piece in key c, which properly is a variant of the form found in the New Version; it does not otherwise occur in the Old

18. all 1 d-m with corona only (A,B,F)/ IV-V 3.1,10.1 om corona (F)/ I 4,10 om slurs (A,F)/ I 7.2 o (A,B,F)/ I 8.5 o (F)/ I 10.4-5 d-qu squ (F)/ III 11.1 om corona (B)/ I 13.4 e" (A,F)/ I 17.4 sharp (F)

19. III 5.2 o (A)/ I 12 om slur (A)/ II 13.2-3 2qu (F)/ V 13-14 om tie (A435)/ I 15.1 d" (A,B,F)/ IV-V 15-16 om tie (A)

20. I 5-6,10,17-18 om slurs except for 5.1-2 (A)/ II 5.6 d" (F)/ II 10.3-4 tie (F)/ II 11.7 a' (A,F)/ V 11.3-4 d-m (F)/ I 12.1-2 slur (F)/ V 16-17 om tie (A)

21. B) gives IIIa, A) gives IIIb. The two may be the sundered halves of a continuous part. Source F) begins with the instruction '8 times &c.', and in line V copies only bars 1-6 (once through the ground, that is); which implies that the piece, one of 24 bars as it stands in all other extant versions, was played the equivalent of twice through. This could accommodate lines IIIa-b serially/ I 11.6 e' (A)/ I 12 corona, followed by double bar (B)/ IIIb 13.1 o (A)

Sett no.4 in D

22. Sources A,B,F
B) has II-III only/ I 5.8 o (F)/ IV-V 5.5 o (A434,436)/ II 12.4 o (A)/ V 16.1,17.1 o (F)/ II 23.1 cr m (B)/ IV,V 23.5-6 o sharp (A434,436)

23. Sources A,B,F
B) has II-III only/ II 4-6 om slur (A)/ III 13.1-2 om tie, m g (A)/ V 16.2 G (F)/ I 22.3 f' (F)

24. Sources A,B,F
B) has I,III only/ I 3,11 om slur (A)/ II 4-5 om tie (A)/ V 15.1 extra sbr a (F only)/ V 19-20,21-22 om ties (A)/ III 20-21 om tie (A)/ V 21-22 om tie (F236)/ I 26.1 c" (F)/ II 27.3 b (A,F)/ I 29 om tie (A)/ V 37.2-38.2 d-m 2qu (F)

25. Sources A,B,F
B) has I,III only/ I 2.4 m cr-rest, om corona (F)/ V 2.4,7.2 cm corona (F)/ V 3.2-4.1 d'c' (F)/ m 5.1 om corona (F451)/ I 12,15-16,18,20-1,23 om slurs (A)/ II 14-15 om slurs om tie (A)/ I 16 om tie (A,F)/ III 17 om tie (A)/ V 19.2-3 tie (F)/ II 20.1,24 om slurs (A)/ III 21 om slur (A)/ V 22 om slurs (F451)

26. Sources A,B,F,M
B) has I,III only/ II 1.4 B (A)/ I 3.3 o (P,M)/ V 5-6 A) has higher notes, M) the lower/ V 11.1 d (M)/ I 15.1 d' (M)/ II 23.1 om (M)/ II 24.1-2 repeated (M)/ V 24.1 cr m dA (M)

27. Sources A,B,F,M
B) has I,III/ 'Cor://:' (A) 'Sarabrand' (F)/ I 1.3 a' (M)/ V 1.2 D (M)/ V 2.2 d-m A (M)/ II 9.4-5 f'g' (M)/ I 10.2 g' (M)/ IV-V 12.1 o (A,F451)/ V 14.3-15.2 m cr d-m Bff (M)/ I 16.1 om (M)/ I 17.1 m cr a'sharp b' (M)/ II 17.3 c" (M)/ I 18.1-2 repeated (M)/ all 18 ends with m (A,M) 2d-m tied (B)

28. Source B(I,III only, II,IV-V editorial)
I 2.2 b'

Sett no.5 in D

29. Sources A,B,F
B) has I,III only/ 'Alman' (F)/ I 1-2 om tie (B)/ II 1-2 om tie (A)/ V 4.1-2,16.1-2 tie (F236)/ I 11-12 tie (F)/ II 11-12 tie (A)/ IV-V 11.7 o (A)/ I 15.2 o (B)/ 21 sbr (B)

30. Source B(I,III only, II,IV-V editorial)

31. Sources A,B,F
B) has II-III only/ I 2.3 o (A)/ II 2.5 om (A,B)/ III 2.1-2 o d-cr qu (B)/ I 3.1-2 d-qu squ (F)/ II 3.3 m (A,B)/ V 8.3,21.3 sbr (F451)/ I 10.2 e" (A) f"(F)/ I 20.6 a" (A) f" (F)/ II 20 om slurs (A,F)/ III 20-21 om tie (A)

32. Sources A,B,F
B) has I,III only/ 'Sarabrand' (F)/ V 1 om coronae (F451)/ I 2.4 om corona (F)/ I 5.2-3,8.2-3 2qu (A) d-qu squ (B)/ I 13.2 o (A,F)/ I 15.4-5 d-m (A) cr-rest m (F)/ III 16.10 o (B)/ I 19 om tie (A)/ III 19.2 2qu (B)/ V 19.2-3 m (F)

33. Sources A,B,F
E) p.91 contains a version in key C for 2B and organ derived from a prior version very close to that of the Old Royall Consort but with a shorter second strain
B) has I,III only/ I 3.6 g" sharp (B)/ III 7.3-4 d-m (B)

34. Source B (II-III only; I, IV-V editorial)
II 'fast tyme'/ II 9.4-10.2 2qu 2cr d-m tie m g"sharp a"b"c"' a"/ III 20.3 c'/ II 21.3 a

35. Sources A,B
B) has I,III only/ II 3.4 sharp (A)

Sett no.6 in D (lacks nos.36,40)

37. Sources A,B,F
    B) has I,III only/ 'Alman' (F)/ II 5.6 c" (A)/ I 10.4 o (A,B)/ I 20.1 o (A)/ III 20.2-3 2qu (A)/ I 26.5 g' (A,B) a' (F)/ III 28.1 d' (B)

38. Source B (I,III only; II,IV-V editorial)
    III 13.6 d

39. Source B (I,III only; II,IV-V editorial)
41. Source B (I,III only; II,IV-V editorial)

41. Black notation/ I 'fast tyme'

Sett no.7 in a (lacks no.42)

Sources A,B

43. B) has II-III only/ II 13.1 om (B)/ II 14.1-2 extra m c" (B)/ IV-V 20.1 tie 2cr cB in the sources/ III 23.1-2 e'd' (A)/ III 24.4 d (A,B)

44. B) has II-III only/ III 1 br-rest (A,B)/ III 4 editorial/ II 17.4 o (A)/ II 21.2 d" sharp (B)

45. B) has II-III only/ all 14-16 [see insert] (A,B) this should probably read like the New Version, but an error at IV-V 15.1 has been compounded by altering first 16.4, then lines I-II, and further adapting III slightly/ III 16.4 c (A,B)

(A, B)

46. B) has II-III only/ III 2.4 o (A,B)/ II 3.4 o (A)/ III 5.5-6 o (A)/ I 14.6 b" (A)/ II 14.3 o (A)

47. B) has I,III only/ III 4.1 natural added (B)/ IV 5.2-3 2qu (A)/ V 5.2 2cr (A)/ III 19.2 o (A)

48. B) has I, III only/ V 6.4 f (A435)/ III 8.5 a (A) c" sharp (B)

Sett no.8 in C (lacks no.49)

Sources A,B (I,III only)

50. V 10.2 b (A435)/ V 40-41 om tie (A435)

51. III 17.4 editorial addition/ III 19.1 cr d' follows (A,B), possibly an insertion after error in bar 17 - it gives 8ve parallel with lines IV-V/ II 26.6-27.1 f'sharp m could be derived from f'o slur f'sharp ; New Version has 2cr here, though lacking slur

52. I 5.10 g' (A,B)/ I-II 12 interchange, by comparison with New Version/ IV-V 18.1 d-m (A)/ III 19.6 f (A,B)/ I 20.12 c' (A,B)

53. I 3.2 f' (A)

54. II 3.5 om dot (A)/ I 7.1 o (A)/ I 8.6 e' (A,B)/ III 8.6 e' (A) d' (B)

Sett no. 9 in F

Sources A,B

55. B) has II-III only/ II 10 om slur (A)/ III 17.4 o (A,B)/ III 1 8.12 o (A,B)

56. B) has I-III only/ I 5.2 o (B)/ II 5.3,5 o (A)/ IV 10-11 om tie (A)/ I 19.5 flat (A,B)/ IV-V 22.1 flat (A)

57. B) has II-III only/ I 4.1 b' (A)/ III 14.1-2 om tie (A)/ III 17.3 om (B)/ III 18.3 m (B)

58. B) has II-III only/ II 11.2-12.1 5cr-rests (A,B) where New Version has 3cr m b'c"d"g'/ II 14.2-4 a'b'c"(A)

59. B) has I,III only/ III 15.4 o (A,B)/ I 19 om tie (A)

60. B) has II,III only/ III 8.2 o (A)/ III 16.7 a (A,B)

Sett no.10 in B flat
Sources A,B

62. B) has II-III only/ III 6.5-8 abc'd' (A,B) altered editorially

63. B) has II-III only/ V 20 om tie (A435)

64. B) has I,III only/ I-II 13.6 d",b' respectively (A)/ II 14.5 o (A)

65. B) has II-III only/ I 6.1 g" (A)/ III 6.1-2 2cr (A,B)/ II 9.5 c" (A)/ III 9.6 o (A,B)/ II 10.1,7 qu,cr instead of cr,qu (A,B)/ IV-V 11.2 e (A)/ III 14.3 f (A,B)/ V 16.2 c (A435)/ II 20.4 e" (A)/ II 20.1-2 d"e" (B)/ III 25.7 o (A,B)

66. B) has II-III only/ I 5.1 natural erased (A)/ I 9.3 b' (A)/ II 13.4-5 d-cr qu (B)

67. B) has II-III only

SOURCE ORDER

For setts
- A): g-G   d   D   a   Bflat   C   F~
- B): g-G   d   D   ~d~   Bflat   F   a   C~

Within setts:
  – = neighbouring in the standard sequence; < = inversion of standard sequence; : = adjacency to related group; / = sett-boundary comparable to standard order; * = unfilled copying area; ~ = break in author-continuity. Numeration within orders d-D derives from the autograph sequence. For the remainder as found in the new version, Och 754-9, Source G, is the guide.

d-order (pieces 2-8,8-13,15-16,18-21)

A): 8		/15-16 18-19-20-21	10	12-13						
B): 8		/15-16 18-19-20	10	12-13~	9	2	11	3-4	21	5-6~
F): 8-9	11	/15-16 18-19-20-21	10	12-13~			11~			
M):			~10	12-13			11~			

D-order (pieces 22-35,37-39,41)

A): 22-23	25	35	24	26-27 /29	31	33	37	32					
B): 22-23	25	35	24	26-27 /29	31	33	37	32	38-39	34	30	41	* 28 *
F): 22 25		:23-24 :26-27		~29	31	33	37	32					
M):				~26-27~									

a-order (pieces 43-48)

Sources invert order for 46-47

C-order (pieces 50-54)

Sources follow standard order

F-order (pieces 55-61)

Sources follow standard order

B flat-order (pieces 62-67)

Sources follow standard order

THE MISCELLANEOUS AIRES for 2Tr-T-B-bc: Critical Commentary

Sett in g

a) 101. Sources A,B,F,T; version in D) and associated sources, for 2B divisions and organ
B) has II-III only/ IV 3.5 o (T)/ III 4.1 sbr (T)/ I 7.1 o (A,F)/ IV-V 7.4 o (A)/ III 10.2 o (A,T)/ all 12 ends with br (T)/ II 14.2 o (T)/ III 14.3 o (A,T)/ I 15.6 o (T)/ III 15.3 o (B,F)/ I 18.5 o (T)/ III 18.3-4 m e (A,B)/ I 18-19 om tie (A)/ III 18-19 tie (B)/ II 19.9 o (A,T)/ III 19.1-4 4qu (A,B)/ IV 19.5 o (T)/ III 20.2 o (A)/ IV 21 sharp erased (A434,436)/ I 23.9 o (T)/ II 23.1 o (A,B,F)/II 23.2 o (F,T)/ III 23.4 o (A,B)/ all 24 sbr (A,B,F)/ III 28-9 om tie (A,B)/ I 29.4 o (F,T)/ I 29.7 qu 2squ b'natural a'b'natural (A,F)/IV 29.1 o (T)/ III 30.2,4 o (T)/ II 32.4 sharp (A)/ II 33.5 natural added (B) o (T)/ I 34.4 o (T)/ IV 34.2-35.1 om (T)/ IV 36.3 o (T)/ I 37.9 d-cr qu a'g' (A,F)

b) 103a. Sources A,B,F,P,T,U; further version in D) and associated sources, for 2B divisions and organ
B) has I,III only; T) has II,IV only/ k-s one flat (U)/ I 2.1-2 om tie (A)/ II 4.5-6 2qu (T)/ II 4.5-6 2qu (T)/ II 12.5 o (T)/ II 12.7-8 om (T)/ IV 14.3 natural (T)/ II 15.1 o (F)/ I 15-16 om tie (A,B,F)/ IV 16 2m dD (A,U)/ IV-V 21.1-2 cr 2qu bBc (A) cr d-qu squ (F,U) d-cr qu bB (T)/ I 22.4-5 2qu (A,T)/ II 27 sbr-rest (T)/ IV 27.2 f (A,F,U) F (T)/ I 28.5 o (A,F)/ II 28.3 extra cr-rest (A,F)/ II 28.4 o (A,F)/ II 28.5,6 cr, om cr-rest (A,F)/ I 29.5 o (A,F)/ I 9.6 o (A,B,F)/ II 29.2 cr (T)/ II 29.4 qu-rest qu (A,F)

103b. Source W
No separate continuo part survives

c) 338. Sources A,B,F
B) has II-III only/ all 7,16 m only (A)/ II 8.2-3 sharp (B)/ II 12.4 o (A)/ II 13.1 sharp (F)/ III 13-14 much erased (A)/ III 13.3 cr m, the cr inserted (A)/ III 14.1,3 inserted (A)

d) 70. Sources A,B,F
B) has II-III only/ II 5.2 o (A)/ I 8.1 tie qu d" (F) II 10.1 o (A)/ III 10.3 subscript sharp erased (A)/ III 11.1 o (A) by confusion with previous bar/ I 18.1 o (A)/ II 23.2 o (F)/ IV-V 23.3 o (A)

e) 339a. Sources A,B,F,M,P,T
B) has II-III only; T) has I,IV only/ black notation (F)/ II 2.2 f" (M)/ I 4.2 d-cr qu c"b' (A,F)/ I 5.6 o (A,F)/ I 6.2 o (A,M) d-cr qu e'd' (A,F,M)/ II 6.1 o (A)/ IV 11.3 d-m (M)/ IV 12.1 cr (M)/ I 13.2 d-cr qu a'g' (A,F,M) slur (F)/ all 13.3 m (A) d-m tie m (B) sbr (T)/ II 14.2,5 o (A)/ I 15.5 o (M)/ I 22.4 m cr-rest (M)/ I 24 divided in half by bar (T)/ III 24.2 a (A) g (B)/ I 25.2-26.3 9cr-rest (T)/ I 29.6 d-cr qu a'g' (A,F)/ all 30 d-m (A,F,M) d-m tie m (B) br (T)

339b. Source W
No separate continuo part survives/ III 18 stemless d-m, or d-sbr, om corona/ III 20.3 / III 34.1 g

f) 337. Source W
No separate continuo part survives; V 6-8,30 continuo line is editorial suggestion/ III 25.1 g'; improbable against a' in line I

Sett in G

g) 79. Sources A,B,F
IV-V 8.5 sharp (A434) sharp added (A435-6)/ V 17-18 tie (F451)/ I 24-25 om tie (A)/ V 24.1 o (F451)

h) 320. Sources A,B,F,M,W
W) has a 3-part version, lacking III and without known continuo, but otherwise comparable/ II 11.3-12.1 d'd' (A,B,F,W) e'f' (M)/ II 15-16 om tie (A,B)/ II 19.4 o (A,B)/ I 22.1 e' (A,B,F,)/ d' (M,W)

i) 80. Sources A,B,F,M
I 3.4 sharp (A)/ IV 4.3 2cr aA (M)/ I 10.2-3 2qu (A)/ I 13.5 e' (M)/ V 18.2 sbr (F451)/ V 23.1 o (F451)/ V 26.2 o (F451)/ II 27.4-5 2squ c"d" (B)/ I 35.2 c' (A)/ II 33.3 o (M)

j) 322-3. Sources A,B,F
B) has II-III only/ black notation (F)/ II 8.1 corona (B)/ II 8.2-5 om slurs (A)/ V 8.3-4 d-m (F451)/ all 10,20 d-m only/ III 12.4 om corona (B)/ II 15.3 g'(A,B,F)/ V 15.1-2 m (F451)/ II 16.3 g" (A) f" (B)

Sett in d

k) 76. Source U
I 5.4 o/ I 6.6 o/ II 6.6 o/ II 7.6 o/ all 11 ends with br/ II 22 sbr/ IV-V 23 br-rest (18943) br-rest beneath line III in basso seguente line (18944)/ IV 29 d-br, dot partially erased

l) 260. Source U
I 7.3-5 *sic*/ I,IV,V 9 br/ I 15.3 g'/ IV 22.2 sharp / I 24 m/ all 34 br

m) 264. Source T
lacks continuo; unascribed/ II,IV om k-s/ II-IV mixed black-white notation/ II 3.5 flat assumed/ IV 4.1 flat/ II 5.2 flat assumed

Further Versions

e) 339a. NYp Drexel MS 5611 f.127; keyboard arrangement by Benjamin Cosin
g) 79. D-Hs (Hamburg) ND VI 3193 no.98 (2Tr-2B?-bc)
h) 320. W) no.9 a3 (2Tr-B); Lbl Add.17792-6 no.21 (2Tr-B); Lbl Add.31423 f.174 (Tr-B) T 302 f.12 (2Tr-B); Hamburg ND VI 3193 no.97 (2Tr-2B?-bc)
m) 264. Lbl Add.10337 f.31 (keyboard); Och 92 f.22 inv (keyboard); Och 1236 f.18v (keyboard); Ctc 0:16.2 p.7 (keyboard); Cul Dd.6.48 f.18 (lyra-viol); John Playford, *The English Dancing Master* (1651) no.17 (violin or viol; line I only); Richard Mathew, *The Lutes Apology* (1652) no.9 (lute). All sources are unattributed apart from Ctc 0:16.2

SOURCE-ORDER Setts in g-G

A):	~101	103	338	70	339	/79	320	80	322-3
B):	~101	103	338	70	339	/79	320	80	322-3
F):	101	339	338	70	103	/79	320	80	322-3 ...
ND VI 3193):						~/79	320		

F) gives the sequence shown above, sandwiched by aires nos. 73 369 370 340 102 341 ... 324 118 325 326. This whole order, including these additional aires, is preceded by the Royall Consort 'Sharpe Aires' selection, and followed by other aires in d,g,G,c,C,D,d also by Lawes.

The Royall Consort
old version

Sett no. 1

(2) Aire [Alman 1]

(3) Alman [2]

(4) Corant [1]

(5) Corant [2]

(6) Saraband

Sett no. 2

(8) Paven

(9) Aire [Alman 1]

(10) Aire [Alman 2]

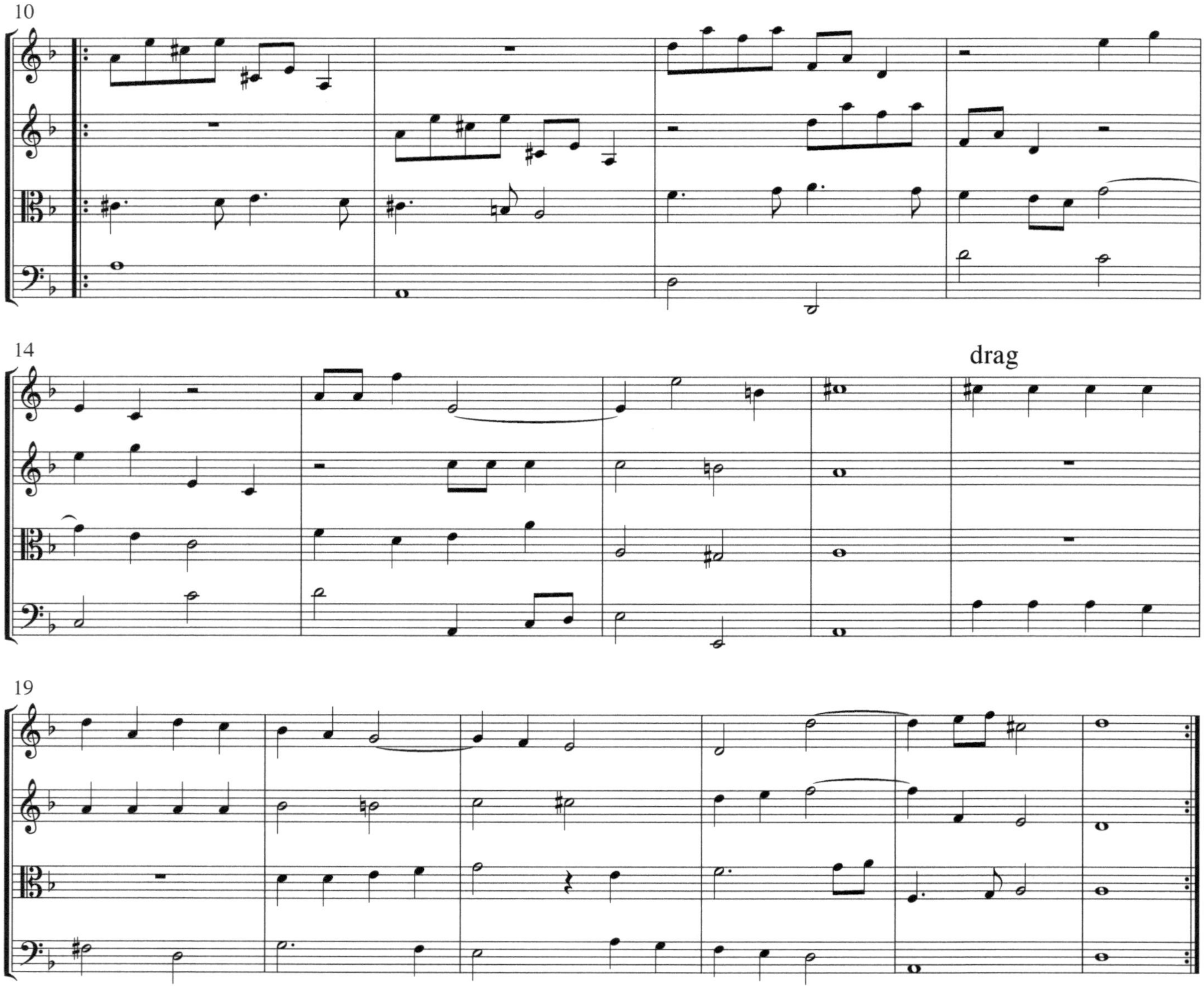

(11) Aire [Galliard]

 William Lawes: The Royall Consort (old version) edited by David Pinto

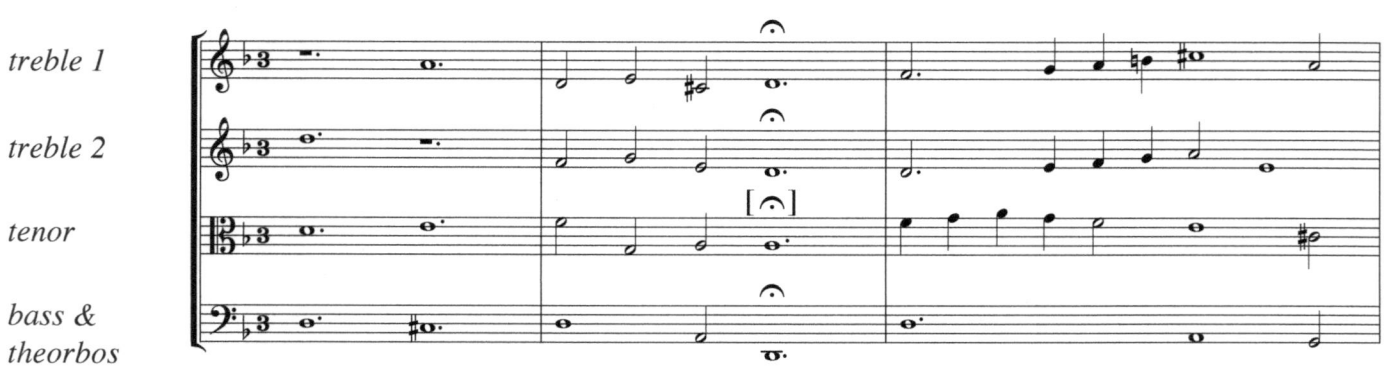

(12) Corant

(13) Saraband

treble 1

treble 2

tenor

bass & theorbos

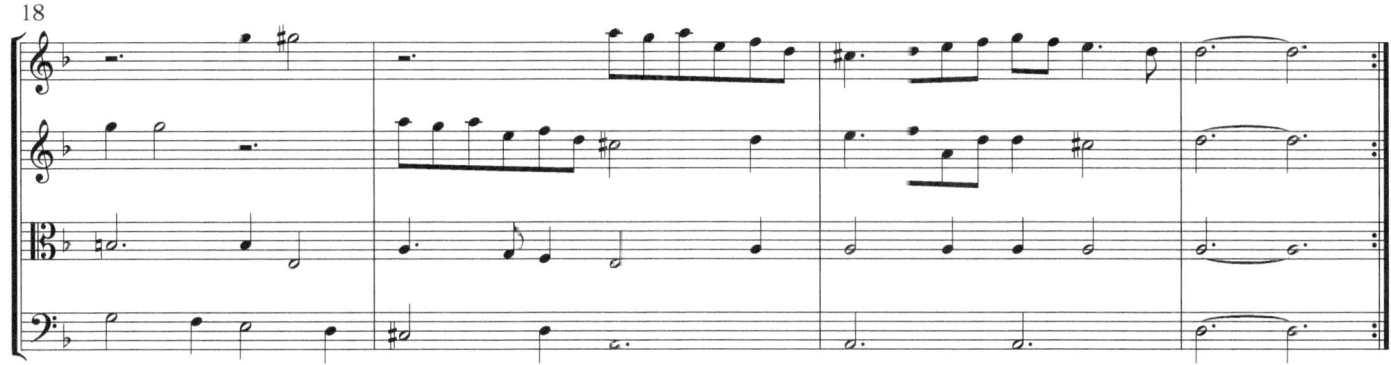

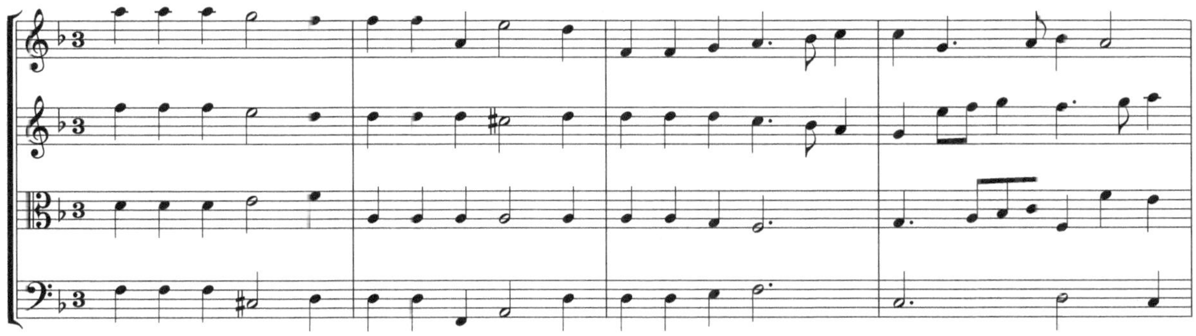

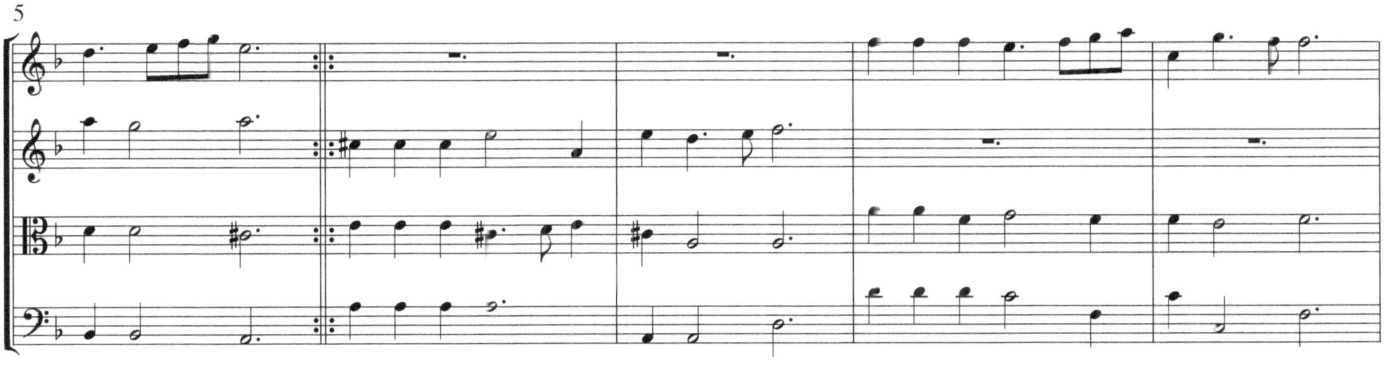

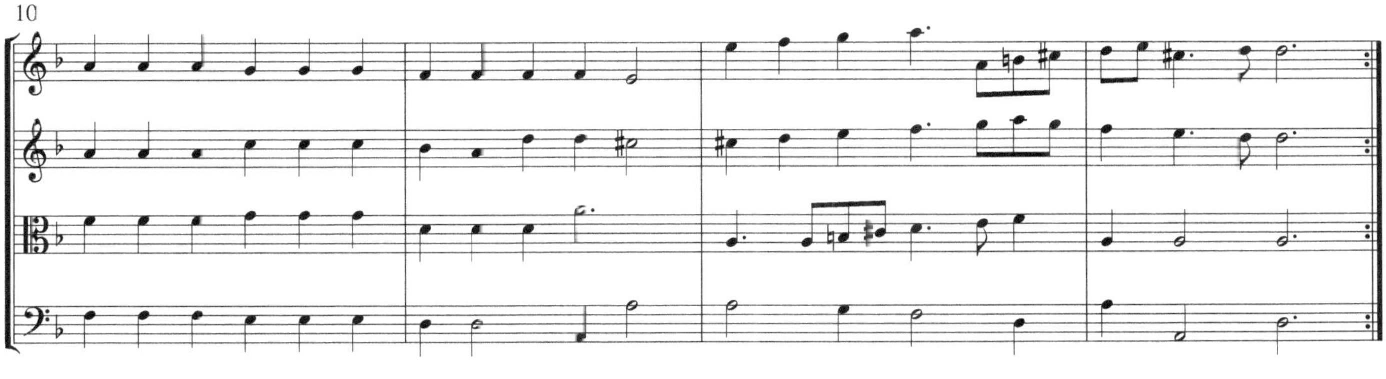

Sett no. 3

(15) **Aire** [Alman 1]

(16) Aire [Alman 2]

(18) Corant [1]

(19) Alman [3]

(20) Corant [2]

(21) Saraband

Sett no. 4

(22) Paven

(23) Aire [Alman 1]

(24) Aire [Alman 2]

© 2004 Fretwork Editions FE12 (2nd edition) William Lawes: The Royal Consort (old version) edited by David Pinto

(25) Aire [Corant 1]

(26) Corant [2]

(27) Corant [3]

(28) Saraband

Sett no. 5

(29) Aire [Paven-Alman]

(30) Aire [Alman 1]

treble 1
treble 2
tenor
bass & theorbos

© 2004 Fretwork Editions FE12 (2nd edition)   William Lawes: The Royall Consort (old version) edited by David Pinto

(31) Alman [2]

© 2004 Fretwork Editions FE12 (2nd edition)   William Lawes: The Royall Consort (old version) edited by David Pinto

(32) Corant [1]

© 2004 Fretwork Editions FE12 (2nd edition)   William Lawes: The Royall Consort (old version) edited by David Pinto

(33) Corant [2]

(34) Aire [Morriss]

(35) Saraband

© 2004 Fretwork Editions FE12 (2nd edition)   William Lawes: The Royall Consort (old version) edited by David Pinto

Sett no. 6

(37) **Aire** [Alman 1]

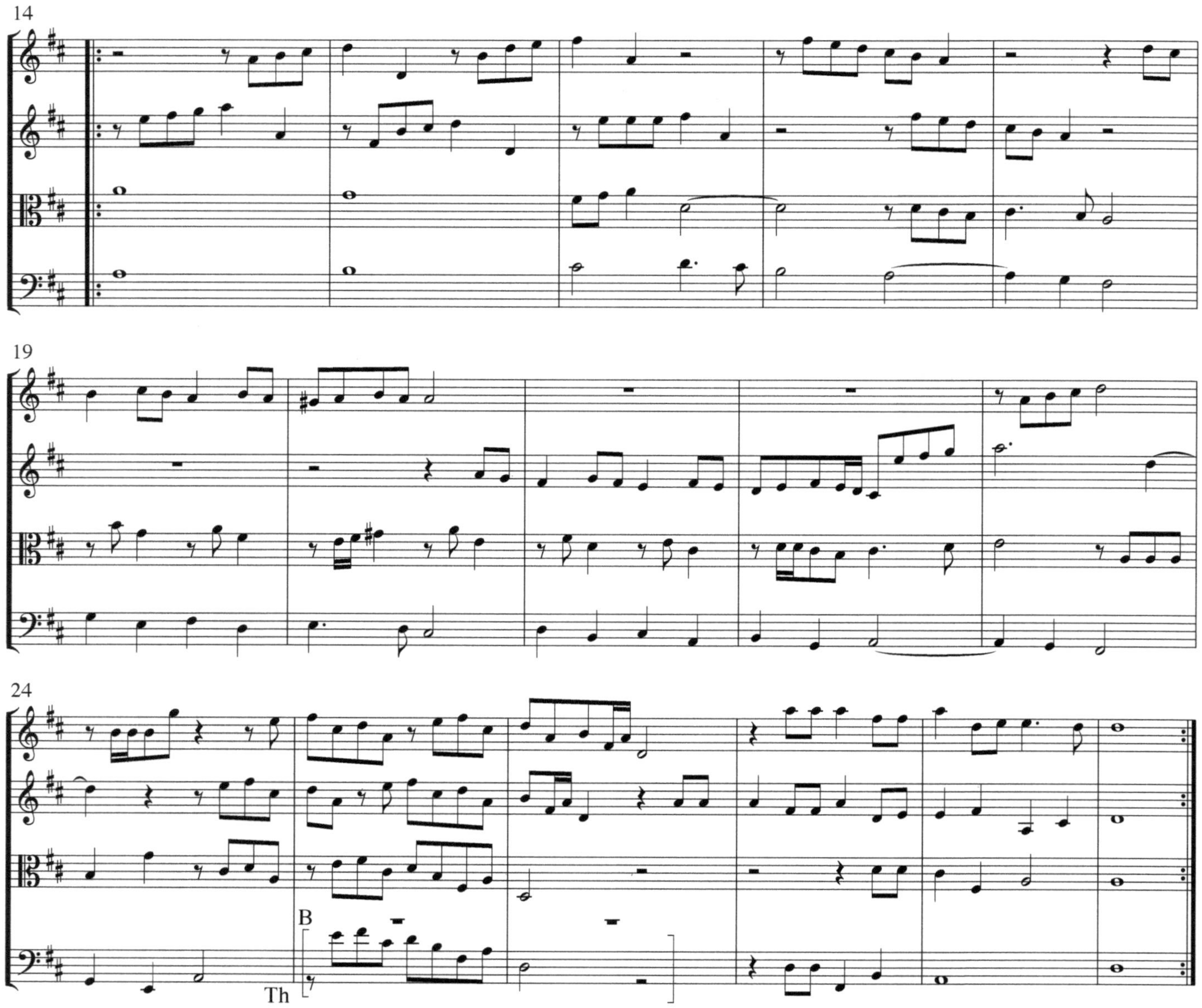

(38) **Alman** [2]

treble 1

treble 2

tenor

bass & theorbos

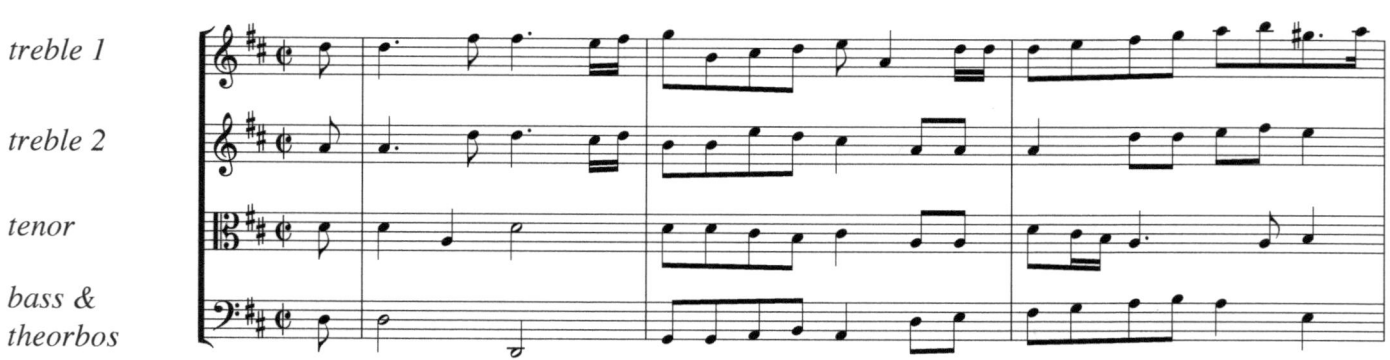

(39) Corant

(41) Aire [Morriss]

© 2004 Fretwork Editions FE12 (2nd edition) William Lawes: The Royall Consort (old version) edited by David Pinto

Sett no. 7

(43) Aire [Alman 1]

(44) Alman [2]

(45) Alman [3]

© 2004 Fretwork Editions FE12 (2nd edition)   William Lawes: The Royall Consort (old version) edited by David Pinto

(46) Aire [Corant 1]

(47) Corant [2]

(48) Saraband

Sett no. 8

(50) Aire [Alman 1]

(51) Alman [2]

(52) Corant [1]

(53) Corant [2]

(54) Saraband

Sett no. 9

(55) Paven

(56) Aire [Alman 1]

(57) Alman [2]

71

(58) Corant [1]

(59) Alman [3]

(60) Corant [2]

treble 1
treble 2
tenor
bass & theorbos

© 2004 Fretwork Editions FE12 (2nd edition)   William Lawes: The Royall Consort (old version) edited by David Pinto

(61) Saraband

Sett no. 10

(62) Paven

(63) Alman [1]

© 2004 Fretwork Editions FE12 (2nd edition) William Lawes: The Royall Consort (old version) edited by David Pinto

(64) Corant [1]

© 2004 Fretwork Editions FE12 (2nd edition)   William Lawes: The Royall Consort (old version) edited by David Pinto

(65) Alman [2]

(66) Corant [2]

(67) Saraband

This page is left blank in order to avoid page turns.

Appendix: The Miscellaneous Aires
[Sett in g]

(101) **Paven**

© 2004 Fretwork Editions FE12 (2nd edition)   William Lawes: The Royall Consort (old version) edited by David Pinto

(103a) Alman

(103b) Alman

(338) Corant

(70) Alman

(339a) **Corant**

treble 1

treble 2

tenor

bass & theorbos

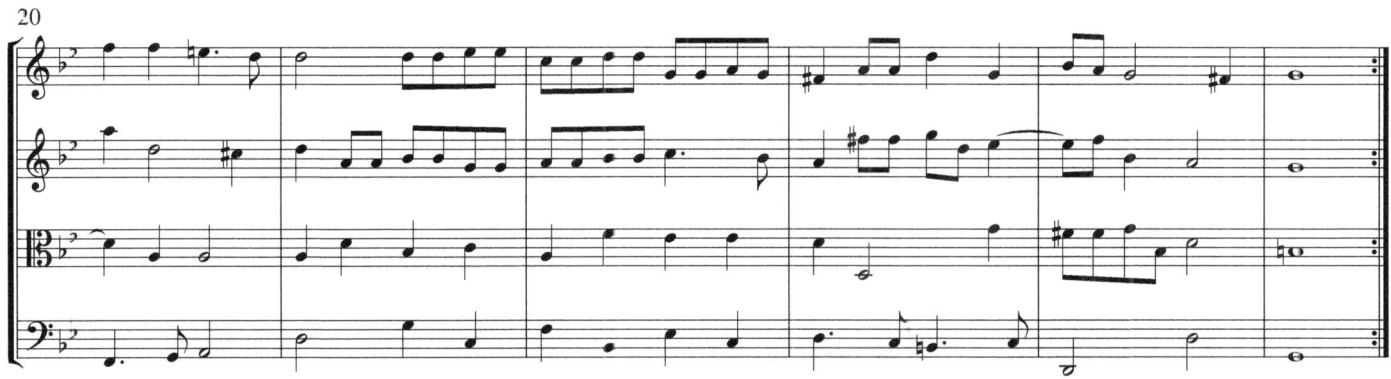

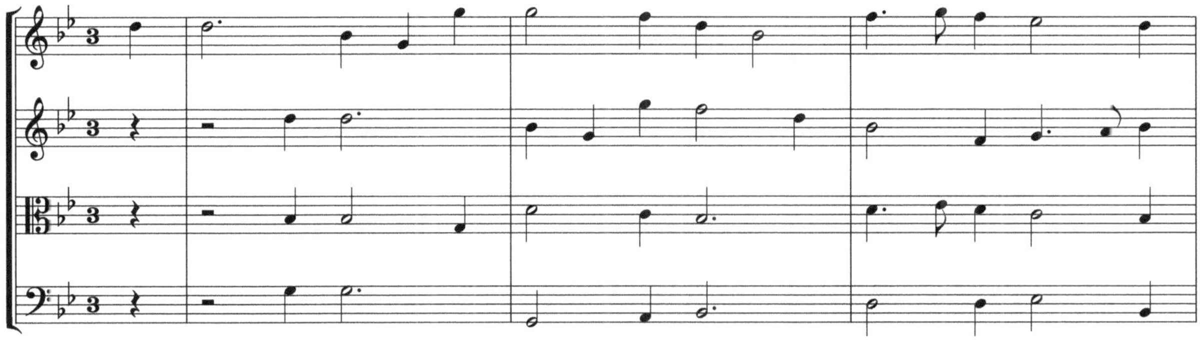

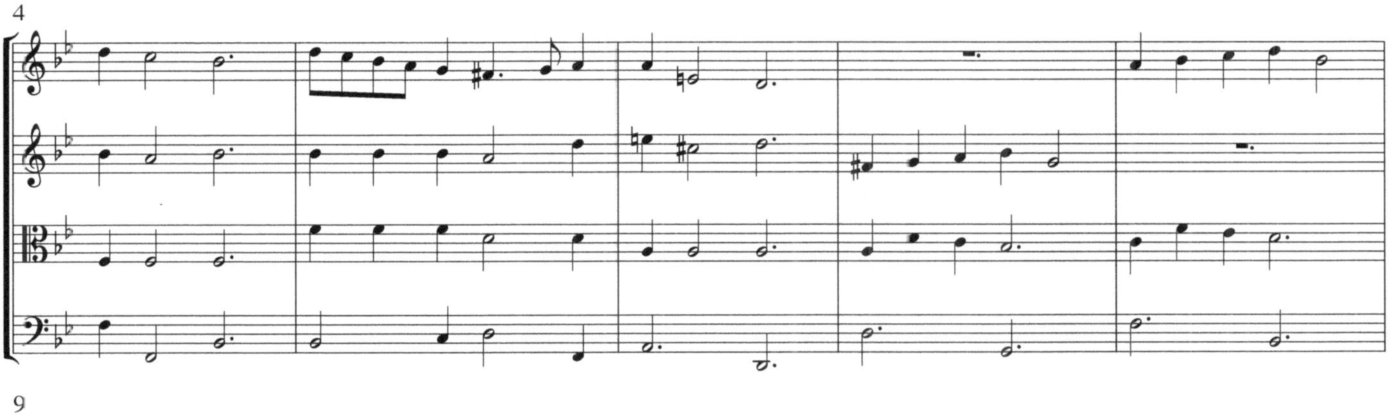

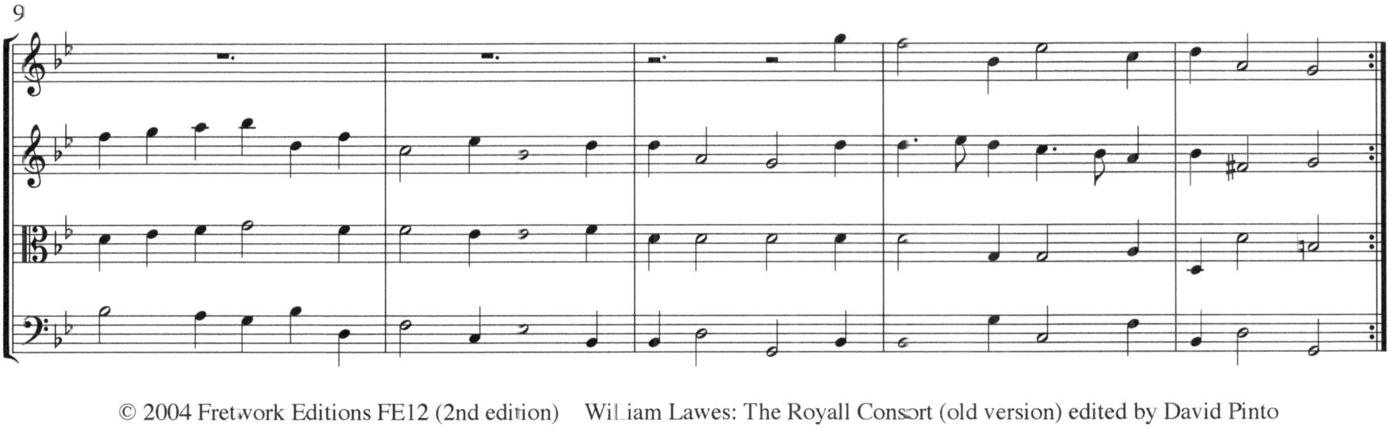

(339b) Corant

(337) Alman

[Sett in G]

(79) Paven

(320) Alman

(80) Alman

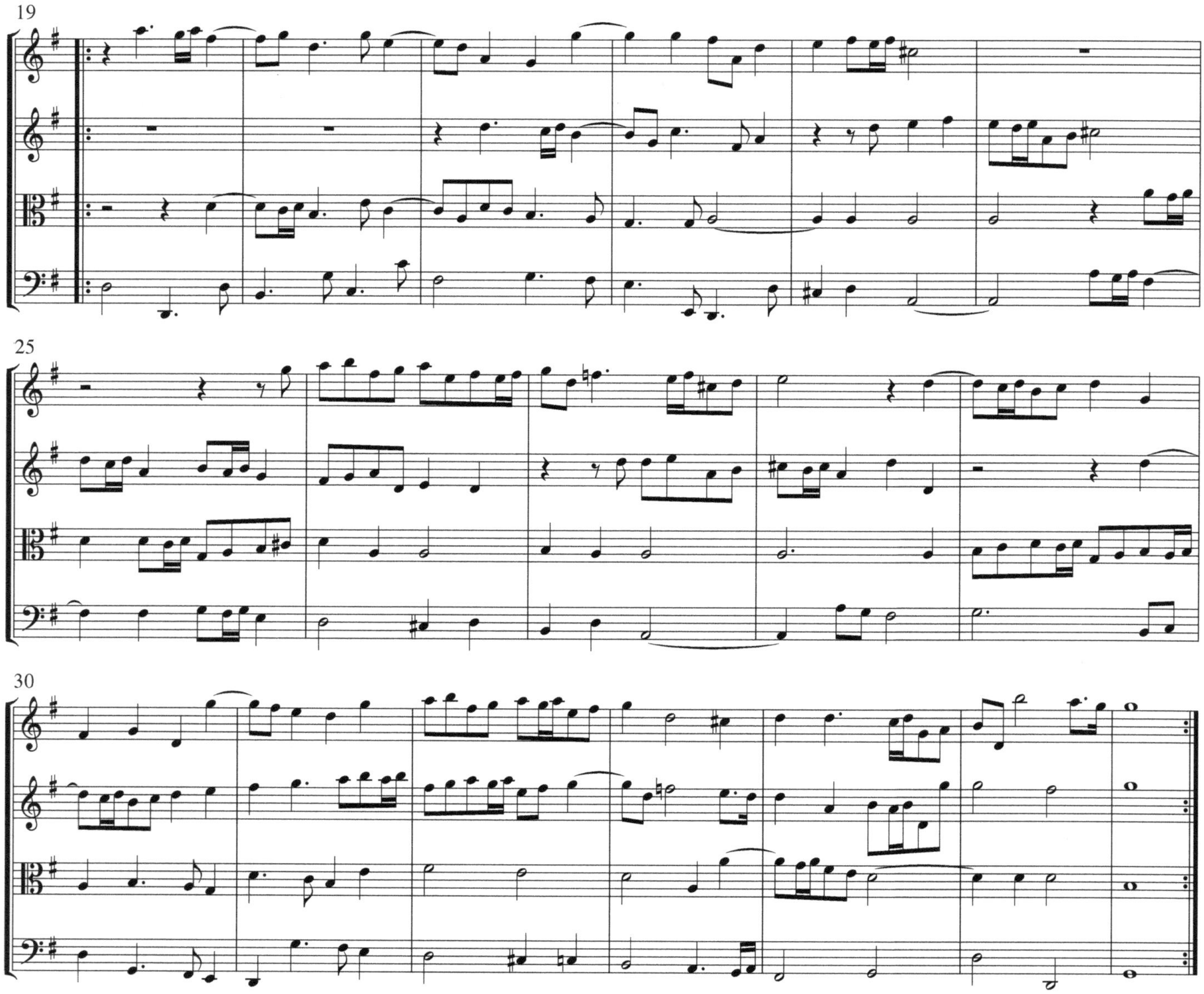

(322-3) **Corant**

 William Lawes: The Royall Consort (old version) edited by David Pinto

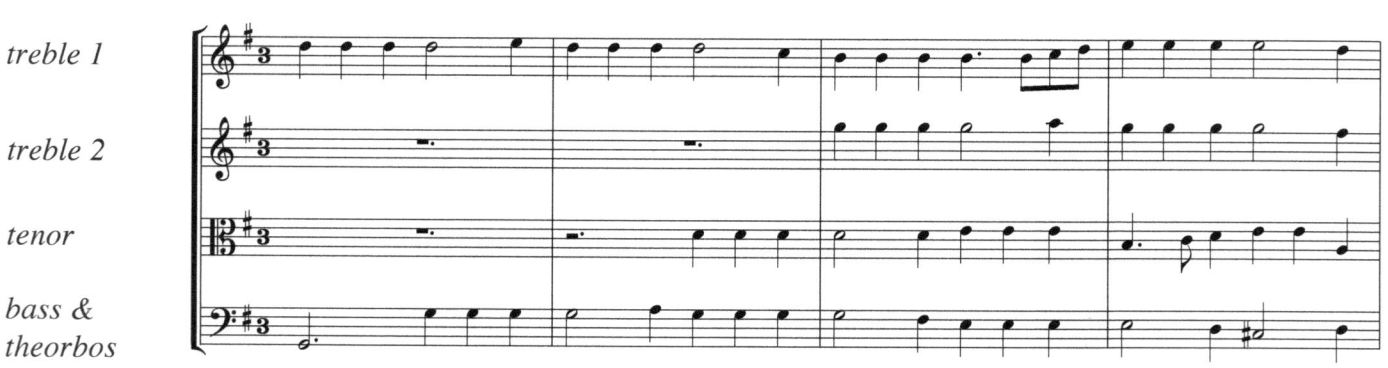

[Sett in d]

(76) Paven

(260) Alman

© 2004 Fretwork Editions FE12 (2nd edition)   William Lawes: The Royall Consort (old version) edited by David Pinto

(264) Saraband

www.ingramcontent.com/pod-product-compliance
Lightning Source LLC
Chambersburg PA
CBHW042017090526
44588CB00024B/2885